Meandering in G

Chapters

(1) Slad Valley 4 miles

(2) Kings Stanley to Ebley Mill 3.5 miles

(3) Amberley 2.5 miles

(4) Wotton under Edge to Tyndale Monument 4.5 miles

(5) Rodbourgh 4 miles

(6) Frampton on Severn 3 miles

(7) Stinchcombe 2.5 miles

(8) Eastington 4.5 miles

(9) Minchinhampton 3 miles

(10) Olveston 3 miles

DISCLAIMER

The contents of the book are correct at time of publication. However we cannot be held responsible for any errors or omissions or changes in details or for any consequences of any reliance on the information provided. We have tried to be accurate in the book, but things can change and would be grateful if readers advise me of any inaccuracies they may encounter.

I have taken every care to ensure the walks are safe and achievable by walkers with a reasonable level of fitness. But with outdoor activities there is always a degree of risk involved and the publisher accepts no responsibility for any injury caused to readers while following these walks.

SAFETY FIRST

All the walks have been covered to ensure minimum risk to walkers that follow the routes.

Always be particularly careful if crossing main roads, but remember traffic can also be dangerous even on minor country lanes.

If in the country and around farms be careful of farm machinery and livestock (take care to put dog on lead) and observe the **Country Code**.

Also ensure you wear suitable clothing and footwear, I would advise wearing walking boots which protect from wet feet and add extra ankle support over uneven terrain.

There are a few rules that should be observed if walking alone advise somebody were you are walking and approximate time you will return. Allow plenty of time for the walk especially if it is further and or more difficult than you have walked before. Whatever the distance make sure you have enough daylight hours to complete the walk safely. When walking along a country road always walk on the right to face oncoming traffic, the only exception is on a blind bend were you cross to the left to have a clear view and can be seen from both directions.

If bad weather should come in making visibility difficult, do not panic just try to remember any features along route and get out the map to pinpoint the area but be sure before you move off, that you are moving in the right direction.

Unfortunately accidents can still happen even on the easiest of walks, if this is the case make sure the person in trouble is safe before seeking help. If carrying a mobile phone dial 999 or 112 European Union emergency number will connect you to any network to get you help.

Unmapped walks we recommend that you take the relevant Ordnance Survey map and compass with you, even if you have a Smartphone, digi-walker or G.P.S all of which can fail on route.

Introduction

Gloucestershire the land of the Cotswolds and open valleys with its colourful tapestry of wild and beautiful meadows. Look out over the many valleys and it is just like time as stood still with the long grass tightly joined to woodland leaving no joins along the way. Then there is the sweet scent of wild flowers in the air, and the striking sound of silence, only the gentle hum of bumble bees or the odd song from the birds. The crops set out a pattern created by a painter with is palate containing every colour you can think of with a dash of sunlight to give you a back drop to remember.

The woods are wild but well managed to help with new growth, there are many different types of trees with the narrow footpaths twisting and turning throughout the woods, and most of these footpaths have been walked for many centuries by monks, poachers and may be Templar Knights.

Slad is one of the first walks I set out on because 2014 was the centennial anniversary of Laurie Lee the poet and author, he wrote about is early years in Slad which was a book called Cider with Rosie, which was also a TV series and a film.

Slad also forms part of what is called the five Golden Valleys which also include Nailworth, Painswick, Cam and Chalford, along with Stroud which at the time was the industrial centre of the Cotswolds. There is a popular circular walk of the Five Golden Valleys of about 21 miles around Stroud and all the valleys but be warned this can be very strenuous.

The Cotswolds is of course the most famous area in Gloucestershire which gets its name because of the band of limestone hills which covers nearly half the county. The Cotswolds is well known for its gentle hillsides or Wolds, fine houses, historic churches, which are commonly known as wool churches and then there is the picturesque villages with their cream colour stone cottages down in the valleys.

When you are out on these walks you will note that Gloucestershire as a diverse geology which helps to create the landscape, flora and fauna has well as its heritage.

To finish this introduction I leave you with the words of Laurie Lee that describes is Slad and Gloucestershire.

"Greener and more decently lush than is decent to the general herbaceous smugness of the English countryside".

Happy Walking.

Meandering in Gloucestershire

Chapter 1 Slad Valley

Park & Start Grid ref;   SO 878087

Distance: 4 miles

Level; Moderate

Time: 2 hours

Terrain: Open fields, tracks and very quiet country lanes

Maps. O.S Explorer 179 Gloucester, Cheltenham and Stroud

Refreshments: Woolpack Inn Slad.

Slad Valley.

Pond down in the dip of the Slad Valley.

Access to start

Exit the M5 motorway at junction 13, and then take the left slip road towards the A419 into Stroud. Continue to follow the A419 through several roundabouts and at Merrywalks turn left on the A46. Then at the next roundabout take the second exit onto the B4070 and stay on that road to reach the Slad Road to then arrive in Slad. Go through the village and up over the steep hill to reach the layby at Bull's Cross.

Places Nearby

Slad is part of the five Golden Valleys which was named due to the monetary wealth created in the processing of wool from the abundance of the supply of water power. The grey stone of Slad is part of the village which is scattered around the south-east slope of a narrow valley, the whole area was brought alive by the poet and author Laurie Lee, famous for his book Cider with Rosie.

Stroud

The four other valleys completing the Golden Valleys are Cam, Nailworth, Painswick and Chalford. Stroud was the industrial centre of the Cotswold, which was built upon the wool industry and today is still very much of a working town.

There is good entertainment, along with coffee shops, pub's and a lot of restaurants.

The Walk

(1)

The walk starts just outside of Slad, at a layby at Bull's Cross. Then from Bull's Cross go to the end of the layby in the direction of Slad and turn left down a tarmac drive. Continue on down to the bottom and then just before some buildings on the right turn left to cross over a stile. Once in the field head off slightly over to the right down the field and then up the other side to reach a gate at the top. At the top go through gate and keep left along a track, and several metres further on it then joins another track at this point keep over to the right before reaching a lane. Turn right onto the lane and follow all the way down to the bottom, passing by a large pond near Steanbridge Mill, if you want a detour into Slad then continue to follow the lane.

(2)

If however you just want to continue the walk, then go to the end of the pond and turn left up to a stile. Cross the stile into a field, then follow the hedge on the right on up to another stile at the top of the field. Then again cross over the stile and continue to follow the path to a stile. Go over stile and carry on through the next field to once again reach a stile. Cross the stile and follow the path as it veers to the right in the direction of a farm. Go through a gate out onto a track, keep over to the right of Furner's Farm then follow curve around to the left. Then after just 30 metres away from the curve turn right over a stile onto a wooded pathway, and after just a few metres go right over a stile into a large field.

(3)

Continue to follow the well-defined path through the field with the farm high up above on the right. At the bottom of the field cross a stile and keep over to the right of a pond. Then once at the top end of pond cross another stile into a field. Keep slightly over to the left, to continue on to reach a gate and a stile. Cross stile then once in the next field continue along the lower section in the direction of a telegraph pole near to a hedge, then turn right to cross over a stile onto a track, then turn to the left to join a lane.

(4)

Turn right on lane and follow on down to the bottom of the valley. At the bottom you then start to climb up slightly on the other side of the lane near the corner of a field next to a cottage where you cross over a stile. The terrain starts to rise up very steeply to yet another stile at the top which leads out onto a road. Turn right on the road and stay on the pavement, then after about 150 metres cross road carefully to a footpath up a steep climb through a wooded section. Then midway up through woods there you meet a junction of pathways, be sure to keep over to the left and continue to follow track to a field. Continue to stay on the track through the field near to the hedge and stay on path as it twist and turns in and out of the woodland. Then after a short climb up through the woods turn right out onto Folly Lane and follow the road to a junction. Turn right if you want to go into Slad at the junction, but to continue the walk go straight ahead onto a path which soon reaches a wooded area. Once in the woods, which as several Laurie Lee Wildlife Way trails with literary post along the way, but for the walk just continue straight on through woods to finally emerge on road near to Bull's Cross.

The track leading on up out the wooded area.

Chapter 2 Kings Stanley to Ebley Mill

Park & Start Grid ref; SO 812035

Distance: 3.5 miles

Level; Easy

Time: 1 hour 30 minutes

Terrain: Fields, canal towpaths and old railway track now a new footpath and cycle track.

Maps. O.S Explorer 179 Gloucester, Cheltenham and Stroud

Refreshments: King's Head

Stroud Waterway Canal and River Frome.

Small Swing Bridge across Stroud Waterway Canal to private residence.

Access to start

Exit M5 motorway at junction 13 and then take the left slip road onto the A419 towards Stroud. Follow A419 into Ryeford and at the first set of traffic lights follow signpost marked King Stanley.

Places Nearby

Stroud

In Stroud there are supermarkets, shops and plenty to do all day long. Check out the Stroud Waterway Canal and the Thames and Severn Canal all of which have great scenery and good walks. Also take a look at the new look Ebley Mill and on the weekend may be take a boat ride on the canal. Also take a look at the Snow Mill where they make the artificial snow for the films like Harry Potter and many Hollywood blockbusters films.

The Walk

(1)

The walk starts from the car park opposite the King's Head pub. Cross the road with the King's Head on your right, and then with the sports club on the left walk down along the edge of the playing field to a floodlight pole. Keep over to the right at the pole and then head diagonally and slightly to the right towards a way marker which directs you down some wooden steps and across a footbridge. Then rise up the slope on the other side to a gate on the left, go through the gate and follow path to another gate at the end of the path. Go through this gate to join the Cotswold Way turning left and follow path down and around to a gate at the entrance to a field. Once through gate go across the grassy field at the back of a housing estate, the field as been cut up by horses making it very uneven ground, but then when you're on top the ridge look out to the left to catch a glimpse of Stanley Mill chimney stack. Carry on to the end of the field to reach a gate at the bottom of the slope, go through gate and turn left to reach the road in just a few metres next to Old Brook House on the right.

(2)

Cross over the road carefully and turning right to continue to follow the Cotswold Way down past Stanley Mill on the left, stay on the pavement to reach a road junction A419 at the end in Ryeford. Cross over road at the pedestrian crossing and turn left up ramp onto Ryeford Road and continue to walk uphill to the canal bridge.

(3)

Turn right down slope just before the canal bridge onto the canal towpath and go past the single swing bridge and double locks to reach Oil Mill Bridge, and then continue on to next bridge to leave the towpath and follow the road off to the right to look at Ebley Mill and surrounding buildings.

(4)

Then to continue the walk, go back to the towpath and return back to Oil Mill Bridge to leave the path at the bridge, up to road and turn right down the slope to see the Snow Mill straight ahead Turn left onto a footpath just in front the Snow Mill and walk a few metres on path before turning right to cross a footbridge next to an old sluice and carry onto go through a kissing gate. Go from here along Lane's Sidings footpath next to the River Frome **(this can be very wet at times and if this is the case then return via the canal)** but if all is well then carry on through the water meadow to reach a kissing gate.

(5)

Go through kissing gate and turn right onto footpath which was once the Old Railway Track. This now tarmac footpath and cycle track runs for about 1 mile in parallel with the A419 road. Continue to follow path through the Community Orchard section and on into Ryeford to the second set of traffic lights.

(6)

Turn left and cross at the pedestrian crossing over the A419 to then retrace your steps up past Stanley Mill on the Cotswold Way, crossing the road to Old Brook House, then on back to the car park opposite the King's Head pub.

Stroud Waterway Canal down towards Ebley Mill.

Chapter 3 Amberley

Park & Start Grid ref; SO 851012

Distance: 2.5 miles

Level; Moderate

Time: 1 hour 30 minutes

Terrain: Open common, grassy and may be very wet at certain times of the year, quiet lanes and tarmac pavements.

.Maps O.S. Explorer 179 Gloucester, Cheltenham and Stroud

Refreshments: Amberley Inn

Amberley looking out over the valley.

Walking down to Manor Court.

Access to start

Exit the M5 motorway at junction 13 and take the slip road to the left onto the A419 into Stroud. Then from Stroud take the A46 south towards Nailworth for about 2 miles. After the Old Fleece Inn at Rooksmoor take the second turning on the left up Culver Hill. Continue to climb uphill for about a mile to arrive at the Amberley Inn where there is free parking nearby.

Places nearby

Woodcester Mansion and park

This is a magnificent 19th century Victorian Gothic work of art, which was abandoned in mid-construction in 1873. It is hidden in a very secluded Cotswold Valley with woods, lakes and paths throughout the area.

The Walk

(1)

The walk starts off at the road side parking area near the Amberley Inn. Then take the level tarmac path to the right of the Amberley Inn go past the bus shelter with the school directly behind you. Continue to follow the path which after a few metres crosses over a lane and passes in front of the Old Wesleyan Chapel. Follow the path as it veers around to the right at the back of the chapel and then continue uphill to the top with the Black Horse Pub on the left. Then just past the Black Horse Pub turn left and almost immediately turn left again at a road junction. Continue to follow the lane at the top of a steep hill before about 300 metres descent after passing the Old Bakery Cottage on right near the junction.

(2)

Continue on down the steep hill for about 150 metres then turn to the right, and continue to the bottom of the hill to reach a road junction. With Hawthorn Cottage directly in front, turn right and follow the lane for about half mile with an undulating road surface. The road then starts to rise gently uphill to finally pass the back of the Bear of Rodborough Hotel, carry on to reach the road junction and turn right, then almost immediately turn right again onto a pavement in front of the Bear of Rodborough Hotel next to a busy main road. Stay on the pavement and walk past the hotel car park then slowly and gently climbing uphill to the common. The pavement then comes to an end with a very bad surface, bear right away from the road onto the grass. Go past the Old Amberley Ridge School on the right as you cross the grass in the direction of Manor Court straight ahead in the distance.

(3)

Just continue to follow the path across the grass past the Manor Court and with the grass uneven and may be wet in places head off in the direction of distant cottages. Just before the cottages keep over to the right at the Memorial Cross. Then cross over in front of the cottages and once near the first house cross lane, this then follows on to another lane taking you back down to the Black Horse Pub. Go past pub turn right and retrace your steps back to the Amberley Inn and the nearby car.

Grass area leading off to cottages on walk.

Chapter 4 Wotton under Edge to Tyndale Monument

Park & Start Grid ref; ST 756931

Distance: 4.5 miles

Level; Moderate

Time: 2 hours 15 minutes

Terrain: Open fields, woodlands and lanes, also a walk along part of the Cotswold Way.

Maps: O.S. Explorer 167 Thornbury, Dursley and Yate

Refreshments: Wotton under Edge cafes, pubs and restaurants.

Tyndale Monument.

Westridge Woods.

Access to start

Exit the M5 motorway at junction 14 and take the left slip road onto the B4509 towards Dursley. Then at next roundabout take the first exit onto the B4058, go to next roundabout and exit at second turning. Then follow signpost into Wotton under Edge to enter Market Street to follow through to The Chippings car park.

Places Nearby

Ancient Ram Inn

This is reputed to be one of the most haunted places in the U.K. It was built in 1145, and it is positioned over ancient ley lines. It has been used for devil worship, a pub and a hideaway for highwaymen. GO if you dare?

The Walk

(1)

The walk starts in The Chippings car park, exit up in the top left hand corner between bollards on the far side of the grass verge. Turn right on road and follow up to the main road junction about 200 metres away. Cross the road carefully and go straight up a steep track, this then becomes a road (Merlin Haven), which after a short distance turns into a footpath leading out onto another road. Stay on the road around to a road junction and turn left, then cross road carefully and continue for a few metres before turning right up a tarmac path next to (Little Acres) to reach a road at the top. Turn left and then almost immediately take the first turning right (Westridge Road). Once at the end of the road take the path to the right of house and then go up through a kissing gate.

(2)

After going through gate turn right after a few metres up through a gap in the hedge to walk along the footpath straight through the woods. Now continue along track and after 200 metres to reach a narrow steep path that climbs diagonally up to the right. The path is opposite a gate marked (private), just continue to climb up path to reach a wide track at top of hill.

(3)

Once at top of hill then turn left onto a well-signposted path (Cotswold Way) and then follow on through Westridge Woods (National Trust). Stay over to the left of the conifer plantation, this popular route passes by the Brackenbury Ditches a prehistoric camp, on the left opposite another conifer plantation.

(4)

At this point you then walk between beech trees then into a large field, just follow the way-markers around to the left to reach the Tyndale Monument. Once at the Monument take time to soak up the spectacular views all the way around the area and down the Severn Vale. Then walk around the outside of the field past the Tyndale Monument and then skirting around the old quarry, keep over to the right when meeting a path up from North Nibley.

(5)

Once returning to the entrance to the field then follow the track to a junction of paths, and then take the third exit with the Cotswold Way out on the right hand route. Then in about 60 metres cross over diagonally left a wide track, and continue on path crossing two more tracks before reaching the Cotswold Way.

(6)

Turn left on track and then after about 100 metres turn sharp left beside a line of conifer trees until you reach another track junction after about 100 metres. Turn sharp right onto track beside a wood, when the wood comes to an end keep on track to a road. Continue on down lane for several metres, and then just before two houses on the left cross a stile on the right near to a gate. Keep over to the right down the field and stay on the well- defined path on the right around the outside of a housing estate. The path then finally reaches a road next to the Old Chapel.

(7)

Go straight ahead down the road with the alms-houses on the left, then at the crossroads go straight across and turn left at the next junction. Then after a few metres turn right up Market Street and back to The Chippings.

Overlooking the Severn Vale.

Chapter 5 Rodborough

Park & Start Grid ref; SO 850051

Distance: 4 miles

Level; Strenuous

Time: 2 hours 15 minutes

Terrain: Canal tow-path, country lanes and open common.

Maps: O.S. Explorer 168 Stroud, Tetbury and Malmesbury

Refreshments: Plenty of cafés pubs and restaurants in Stroud.

River Frome.

Thames and Severn Canal tow-path

Access to start

Exit the M5 motorway at junction 13, then take the slip road towards Stroud on the A419. At the next roundabout take the 3rd exit still the A419 then go through 5 more roundabouts. Once in Stroud turn right and exit first exit on roundabout onto Newton's Way then at next roundabout exit at first junction, follow road around to the left to roundabout and take second exit past supermarket entrance to enter public car park.

Places Nearby

Barrow Wake

This is a popular viewpoint in the Cotswold area overlooking the Malvern Hills, Severn Vale and Forest of Dean. One of the plaques in the car park says over 500 million years of Britain's history.

The Walk

(1)

The start of the walk is at the car park just off London Road, adjacent to Waitrose car park. Leave the car park at the exit and follow the pathway down to the right side of the Superstore to steps at the end of store then follow down to Newton's Way bypass. Cross the bypass at the pedestrian crossing and go right on opposite side of road, carry straight ahead under the viaduct and then just a few metres further on take the path to the left. There has been a lot of restoration done in this area and most of it is now finished around the Thames and Severn Canal. Once on the path down to the left follow the canal bank down to the River Frome and then cross a wooden bridge, after about 10 metres up a slight slope take a right turn up to a gate. Go through gate into a field and follow the well-defined path on up to a kissing gate in the top right hand corner. Go through the kissing gate and ignore path to the right continue straight ahead through the spinney and then up a few steps through a gate out to the edge of a football pitch. Follow pitch around the left edge, then on up to the left of a playground out into a car park, still keeping over to the left then straighten up and head for a path with an open white gate which runs between two walls, follow the path up to the top to another gate, go through and take care to cross a busy road.

(2)

Once across road follow the lane down to the right marked Tabernacle Walk leading down into Tabernacle be sure to look at the views on the right out towards the River Severn and beyond, carry on past the church down on the left and then 300 metres further down the lane just before a steep hill take the kissing gate on left that leads into a large field. Descend down the field and head towards the stile straight in front, cross the stile and then go through a small enclosed pathway and exit via another stile onto a road. Turn left on road and then almost immediately turn left again and go through a metal squeeze stile into a field. Keep to the right of the field and continue up a steep climb on the path heading finally to the top left hand corner to a stile with a cottage over on the right.

(3)

Cross the stile and turn right along a path soon to join a metalled road then on up to a crossroad, carry straight across at crossroad up another metalled road and then at the bend in road go straight on ascending up to Rodborough Common, then at a junction in the path keep left passing a seat marked (Shelia Smith) on the right. Then continue to climb common path over to the right and slightly in diagonal direction to a waymark on a stone water trough. At the water trough you can then pick-up the path through the houses, but first cross the stone stile and then follow the path between the houses to reach the estate road. Go straight ahead at road down towards an electrical sub-station keep over to the left at sub-station on to a narrow path and follow straight through to a stile at the end.

(4)

Once over the stile this then takes you back onto the common, keep to the right and follow path in a diagonal manner to reach a road. At this point cross two busy roads with care and head towards a low concrete building (Ice Cream Factory and shop). Walk past the front of the ice cream shop and then after just a few metres turn left down a bridleway which drops steeply downhill, then mid-way down go through a gate to join a lane. Cross over lane to another pathway slightly off to the left and follow down to railway crossing **(Take extreme care crossing the track)** then once on the other side of track on the lane cross over the canal bridge.

(5)

Once over the bridge double back under the canal bridge and follow the tow-path back into Stroud, back next to the viaduct, then head back to the pedestrian crossing retracing your steps back up to the car park.

View out to River Severn.

Chapter 6 Frampton on Severn

Park & Start Grid ref; SO 752089

Distance: 3.5 miles

Level: Easy;

Time: 1 hour 30 minutes

Terrain: Canal tow-paths, riverbank, open fields and country lanes

Maps: O.S. Explorer OL14 Wye Valley and Forest of Dean.

Refreshments: The Bell Inn.

Saul Junction.

The single path from the concrete bridge over the River Frome.

Access to start

Exit junction 13 off the M5 motorway, left at the slip road towards Stroud. At the roundabout take the first exit onto the A419, then at the next roundabout take first exit onto the A38. Follow road for a few miles to take a right turn onto B4071 Perry Way and then next right onto Whitminster Lane to arrive in Frampton on Severn. Just before the Bell Inn on left, take the lane on the right and follow lane around to Saul Junction car park.

Places Nearby

Saul Junction

This place is a haven for narrow boats both linked to the Gloucester and Sharpness Canal and also the Stroud Waterway Canal. There is at Saul Junction a Cotswold Canal visitor's centre and canal shop full of great gifts. There are at certain times boat trips on the Gloucester and Sharpness Canal which are well worth the trip.

The Walk

(1)

The start of the walk is at the car park alongside the Gloucester and Sharpness Canal at Saul Junction. Exit car park in the direction of Gloucester along the canal to Junction Swing Bridge a pedestrian crossing over the Gloucester and Sharpness Canal and then walking past the Old Toll House on the Stroud Waterway Canal. Follow the tow-path to the end past the Saul Junction Marina, to reach the road, cross over the road and go straight ahead over a stile on the opposite side of road and walk along the slightly overgrown section of the Stroud Waterway Canal. If this is very over grown then the alternative route is to turn left and follow road around bend for about 250 metres and then turn right through a large metal gate on the right. Then just follow the track with the River Frome on the left soon to pick-up the junction of the path from the canal. Then follow the single path off to the left as it narrows and twist along the River Frome bank through the meadows and then in through a woodland area. Once out of the wooded section stay on riverbank path to reach a concrete bridge over the River Frome.

(2)

Do not cross bridge but look out to the right over the field at the tractor marks, they are double wheel tracks but select the single track which stands out on its own, this goes off diagonally to the right and slightly across the field to disappear behind a hedge that stands out in the field. Follow the track around a bend and then head for a gap in the hedge with a footbridge through the centre.

(3)

Once through hedge set out again diagonally to the right through the field for a short distance heading again for a gap in the hedge and over a small footbridge. Then follow the hedge up the field and around to the right, then continue on up to the top of the field ignoring gateway on the left. Follow the hedge around field to the right and go over a stile to reach a track which then leads out to a road.

(4)

Cross road with extreme care, then go through small gate to the left of the large park gates and garden centre entrance. Once through small gate then cross the field to the end in the direction of a cottage in the distance, once near the cottage do not exit the small gate marked (private) but turn right to follow the fence down to a gate in right hand corner of the field. Go through the gate out onto a track and follow out to reach a road. Cross the road and then go across one of the longest greens in England. Keep going right over the green to reach a pavement on the far side and then turn right to follow down past the Bell Inn in the far left, next to the road. At the main road, turn left and follow the road for about 250 metres to reach Fretheme Swing Bridge, then once over bridge turn right onto the Gloucester and Sharpness Canal to return to the car park at the start near Saul Junction.

Gloucester and Sharpness Canal.

Chapter 7 Stinchcombe Hill

Park & Start Grid ref; ST743983

Distance: 2.5 miles

Level: Easy

Time: 1 hour 30 minutes

Terrain: paths and walkways throughout woodland and extensive views in all directions

Maps: O.S Explorer 167 Thornbury, Dursley and Yate

Refreshments: Plenty of cafes, pubs and restaurants in Dursley.

Just one of the views from Stinchcombe Hill.

Severn Vale.

Access to start

Exit the M5 motorway at junction 16 and take the left slip road to A38 towards Filton and Thornbury. Then at the roundabout take the first exit onto the A38 Gloucester Road. Continue to follow the A38 for several miles before taking the road on the right signposted Dursley. Once in Dursley follow the signpost to Stinchcombe and the golf course, this road is extremely narrow in places and very steep.

Places Nearby

Jenner Museum

The Dr Edward Jenner museum is in Berkeley, visit the house of this very brilliant man who pioneered the smallpox vaccination. Take a tour of the house, or just down the road explorer the medieval Berkeley Castle.

Newark Park

Newark Park stands high on the Cotswold escarpment looking down over the Ozleworth Valley and further on to the Mendips. Look up the story of Newark founded by an influential English courtier to Henry VIII in 1550, it has since gone through many phases but it is now owned by the National Trust.

The Walk

(1)

The walk starts from the car park looking out over the Severn Valley. Exit car park in the direction of seats overlooking the valley, then turn right until you are insight of the Cotswold Way marker. Turn left at this point and then follow the Cotswold Way path around the upper edge of Hollow Combe keeping the golf course on your right. Go between the woods and the sixth tee up over slope overlooking Stancombe Park, then turn right and continue along the path which leads up to Drakestone Point near a seat.

(2)

Once at Drakestone Point the views are quite magnificent out to the Tyndale Monument, Cotswold escarpment and the Severn Bridges. Drakestone Point was thought to have once been a site of a hill fort. Berkeley Castle cannot be seen from this point anymore due to the additional growth of the trees obstructing the view. But to continue on the walk follow the path back along the top of the hill and past the seat which stands as monument to Sir Stanley Tubbs who kindly gave the hill to the public in a trust just for recreation. Just stay on the path onto Trig Point and the Topograph, then veer slightly to the left and follow the path onto the Tubbs Memorial shelter.

(3)

Continue the walk on the path around the shelter, and then after about 60 metres follow the Cotswold Way marker on the right along the left edge of the golf course. Then continue to stroll on past the eleventh and twelfth tees to reach what is known as the mounting stone. The stone was used to remount the horses on the London Road after walking up the long hill, this was the coach road from Berkeley Castle to London.

(4)

Turn right onto the Coach Road and then veer left to follow the path along the edge of the woods on your left. Go straight across the metalled driveway in front of Stinchcombe Hill House, and then cross the grassland with great views on the left across the River Severn and out over to the Forest of Dean. Then enter the woods and go straight ahead continuing along the path to reach another viewing point out over to Dursley. Also from this point you can see Downham Hill, Uley Bury and the Cotswold escarpment. Continue on down the path, still high up in the woods on the left, and ignore the track that runs off down into the woods. Then pass between the groundsmens hut and the eighteenth tee and continue on across the open grass to reach the golf clubhouse.

(5)

Go past the clubhouse and then turn right to follow the waymarker path, go across the road with care, and then follow the path towards the woods straight ahead. Do not enter woods but just in front of woods take the path off to the right. Then follow path along the edge of the hill back to the car park.

Views out over to the River Severn in the distance.

Chapter 8 Eastington

Park & Start Grid ref; SO 778053

Distance: 4.5 miles

Level: Easy

Time: 1 hour 45 minutes

Terrain: Open fields, country lanes and tracks

Maps: O.S Explorer OL14 Wye Valley and Forest of Dean

Refreshments: Kings Head in Eastington.

Open fields outside Eastington.

Views up towards Coaley Peak.

Access to start

Exit the M5 motorway at junction 13 and take the slip road off to the left to A419 on towards Stroud. Then at the next roundabout take the 3rd exit onto the A419, then at next roundabout take 4th exit onto Spring Hill. The road then further on changes to Alkerton Road, just continue to the end and park near the local shop.

Places Nearby

The Museum in the Park

The Museum in the Park is at Stratford Park in Stroud. The history of the museum dates back to the 1900's when the initial focus was on the natural history and geology but now today it is a much wider history of the district.

The Walk

(1)

The walk starts in Alkerton road where you can park in road near the local store. Walk back down to the roundabout with the Kings Head pub on the left across the road, and turn right away from pub heading in the direction of the M5/A38. After just 20 metres up road turn left down a track between houses marked with a public footpath sign. Go up the track and cross a stile at the end into a field and continue to follow the hedge on the left down to the bottom of the field in the left hand corner to another stile. Cross the stile into the next field and then follow the right hand hedge to the bottom right corner and cross yet another stile.

(2)

Again cross the stile and follow the well-defined footpath diagonally across the field to a footbridge which lines up with a pylon, cross footbridge and then follow the right hand hedge on past the pylon and the next gate on the right, and head for gate in the far right corner. Go through gate turn right and follow the hedge on the right, and then through another gate and on to and over a stile. Once over the stile continue to a gate tucked away in the right hand hedge, it is important not to miss this section because you can go straight ahead ending up miles out of your way. So once through the gate turn halfway to the left and cross the field diagonally to a stile about 10 metres from the corner of the field.

(3)

Again cross the stile and still continue in a diagonal direction across the field towards some buildings with a white thatched cottage at the right hand end. Go around cottage to the right and exit out onto the main road.

(4)

Cross the main road carefully and go over a bridge/stile and veer off to the left across the field heading for the corner of a small copse and a footbridge. Go over the footbridge and then climb up the slope in the field and cross a stile to the left of a large tree. Then go across the next field to a stile but **do not cross** this stile, just turn right and follow hedge to a stile set back in the corner. Cross stile and go straight across field to the edge of Five Acres Grove, keeping around to the left of the Grove and then go between two copses to cross a small field to a gate. Once through the gate turn right and continue to follow the hedge down to reach the railway fence.

(5)

Turn left and follow the fence, onto a track towards the railway viaduct. At this point cross over the river bridge and then turn left into a meadow before the viaduct and then follow the track diagonally back across meadows for about a mile finally to reach a large metal gate next to a small gate, go through small gate out onto a road.

(6)

Turn left onto Millend Road to walk up past Beard's Mill which has now been renovated, and continue to follow Millend Road for about a mile to reach a road junction, this is at the change of roads from Alkerton Road to Spring Hill. Turn left at junction and follow Alkerton Road back into Eastington and your parked car.

Beard's Mill.

Chapter 9 Minchinhampton

Park & Start Grid ref; SO 871008

Distance: 3 miles

Level: Easy

Time: 1 hour 30 minutes

Terrain: open common, tracks and quiet country lanes through small hamlets.

Maps: O.S. Explorer 168 Stroud, Tetbury and Malmesbury.

Refreshments: Plenty of coffee rooms and pubs in Minchinhampton.

Iron Age Bulwarks Minchinhampton Common.

Narrow stone pathway.

Access to start

Exit M5 motorway at junction 13 off the slip road on left and head to A419 and Stroud. Then at the next roundabout take the 3rd exit onto the A419, from here pass through 5 roundabouts but stay on the A419. Then at the next roundabout take the 3rd exit onto A46 Dudbridge Hill. Keep over to the right to stay on the A46 Dudbridge Road, then turn left onto Bear Hill. Turn right then almost immediately turn left onto Windmill Road the road name then changes to West End, to arrive in Minchinhampton. Go through centre onto the High Street to war memorial and turn left onto Bell Lane to car park at the back of the church.

Places Nearby

Minchinhampton Common

The Common is renowned for its rare orchids and its historic grazing rights. It is surrounded by many National Trust areas which include Ebworth Estate, Harefield Estate, and Chedworth Roman Villa, Selsley Common plus many areas of untouched Cotswold countryside.

The Walk

(1)

The walk starts in a free car park at the back of the church in Bell Lane. On leaving the car park and with your back to the churchyard, take the private driveway on the left, this is wedged between the common and houses on the other side of the drive. Then once at the end of the drive continue to follow the path on the common to reach Browns Road, go straight across road and continue to follow the pathway between the houses and the Iron Age Bulwarks on the right. Then follow the stone wall to reach Westfield House, when the wall turns to the left then you continue straight ahead across the common to reach a large roadside house named Windmill Lodge.

(2)

After crossing the road you will then come into contact with a stone wall again on the left, follow the wall straight ahead for about 180 metres as it starts to drop downhill it then starts to sweep around to the left. Stay on the path and after about another 100 metres you pass a stone stile set in the wall on the left which leads into a playing field marked (private). Just follow the wall still slightly downhill towards two large trees and a seat next to a road. Turn left down at the road and continue for about 40 metres before turning right down a driveway towards a house at the bottom. Once at the bottom then head for the house with the eight elongated windows, this once belonged to Edward Payne the stain glass artist. To continue on with the walk head to the right corner of the house and cross a stone squeeze stile.

(3)

This narrow pathway then takes you down a walled path to emerge through a second squeeze stile onto a road, in the village of Box. Turn left on the road and continue to follow around to pass the church on the right, then after a further 250 metres stay on the road as it veers around to the left, but then almost immediately on the curve take the first right down a track signposted to Longford. This track soon turns to the left and gets narrow to go through a low kissing gate, then just follow the path through several kissing gates, taking time to look at the splendid views out over to Gatcombe. At the last of the kissing gates you enter a small paddock keep over to the right and exit a gate at the far end onto a metalled lane at Forwood.

(4)

Turn right on the road and then after just a few metres turn first left, at the bottom of the hill, then follow the road down to a road junction and turn left again. Then from the lane you can look up and see Minchinhampton perched on top of the hill, but this means the only way is up. Once you have climbed the steepest section of the hill continue along the pavement to the crossroads. At the crossroad go into the High Street and walk on up to the war memorial, then turn left into Bell Lane and follow back around the church to the car park.

Views out over Gatcombe with the horse trails up on the horizon.

Chapter 10 Olveston

Park & Start Grid ref; ST 600869

Distance: 3 miles

Level: Easy

Time: 1 hour 30 minutes

Terrain: open fields, tracks and quiet country lanes going through small hamlets.

Maps: O.S. Explorer 167 Thornbury, Dursley and Yate

Refreshments: Plenty pus in Olveston or Tockington.

View out towards the Severn Bridge.

A strange stone stile built into the hedge.

Access to start

Exit the M5 motorway at junction 16, take the slip road on the left to A38 for Filton/Thornbury, and at the roundabout take the 1st exit onto A38 Gloucester Road. Turn left after about 1.5 miles down to Fernhill, then turn right onto Lower Tockington Road follow road around to the right. Then turn left and almost immediately turn left again onto Upper Tockington Road the road changes name to New Road and changes again to The Street to arrive in Olveston then head for the church to park car.

Places Nearby

Slimbridge Wetland Centre

This visit is great for all the family with wildlife and lakes in a beautiful setting. The whole area is managed for a reason to help the wildlife in their natural habitat. Please check the website for more details, you will not be disappointed.

The Walk

(1)

The walk starts by parking in the area of the church or White Hart pub. Then walk down Church Hill between the pub and the church and follow the lane as it leaves the village. Continue to follow the lane for several hundred metres on past a road junction on the right and a sub-station on the left, continue to follow on the lane known as the Common. The road after 250 metres goes past the sub-station which then turns into a track, and the track at the end then veers to the left and crosses a bridge. Once over the bridge the track then swings off to the right and at this point go to the left and through a kissing gate set back in the hedge. Follow the hedge on the left up through the field to another kissing gate, go through gate and turn left and continue to follow the path on through the next two fields. Then at the end of the second field cross a stile and follow path down to the left edge of the field and follow the path through the hedge and cross a bridge over a stream to continue on between a fence and the stream.

(2)

Continue to follow this path at the back of houses, cross over two wooden stiles and then finally reach a stone stile, cross over stile to reach a road. Turn left on the road and go past Deny's Court on the left and carry on to the road junction. Turn right at the road junction and then continue to follow the road out of the village. At the second turning on the left marked Haw Lane, turn down lane and follow the lane up to Orchard Rise on the left. Just past Orchard Rise on the opposite side of road turn up right on to path through a gate set back in the hedge. Follow path up through field keeping over to the left hand hedge in the first field, go through a gateway in to the second field and stay near the right hand hedge and keep to the right in third field.

(3)

About halfway down the third field look out for a stone stile on the right set well back in the hedge. Cross the stone stile and follow the narrow path between fences, then after about 30 metres this then narrow path turns into a track which you continue to follow into Tockington. Once at the road in the village cross over the road, and go down a **No Entry** road directly opposite and continue to follow road down slope to where the road veers around to the right, and at this point at the start of the curve there are two public footpath signs pointing to the left, take the first path and follow path through what was Brook Farm which has now been renovated into houses. Just follow the track through the centre of the buildings along the drive to a gate, go through gate to another gate and then continue to follow the path through a field.

(4)

Follow the path straight across field on a well-defined path in the direction of a stile on the far side of the field. Cross over the stile and then cross a second stile after a few metres into another field and then turn left. Follow the left hand hedge to reach two large gateways, go through the first of these gateways and keep around to the left edge of the field, continue to walk up the field to a kissing gate in the top left hand corner. Go through kissing gate and keep over to left through a playing field with rugby post on your right, carry on up to another kissing gate which you exit on to the road.

(5)

Turn left on road and follow back into Tockington, back past Haw Lane this time on your right and then past Deny's Court at this point keep over to the right and follow the signpost back the quiet country road for about a mile staying on the pavement back into Olveston and return to the car.

Olveston Church.

Chapter 11 Days Inn Michaelwood

Days Inn

This is one of the best positioned hotels to set out and do the walks in the Meandering in Gloucestershire walking book, it is directly off the M5 motorway north bound, but once you have booked in then you can use the back entrance that gives you easy access to the A38 and all destinations.

Enjoy ample free parking, 24-hour reception and unlimited free Wi-Fi Internet access throughout r the Michaelwood hotel, as well as an adjacent Starbucks. Each of the comfortable en-suite guest rooms offers a Hypnos bed, flat screen Freeview television, complimentary hot drinks tray and hairdryer, and you are offered dedicated executive and smoking rooms upon request. For added value, children 12 and under stay and eat free when staying with a paying adult at our pet-friendly hotel in Michaelwood, UK.

LOCAL ATTRACTIONS

Explore all the best Southwest UK attractions from our Gloucestershire hotel. See one of the most famous sites in the world when you visit Stonehenge, a prehistoric monument thought to be constructed in 2400 BC, and the remains of a ring of standing stones set amongst the densest complex of ancient monuments in all of England. See a horse race at Newbury Racecourse, one of the UK's top sporting venues and home of the Lockinge Stakes. Spend an idyllic afternoon at Cotswold Wildlife Park and visit with giraffes, anteaters, lions and dozens of other mammals, reptiles and birds and stroll through 160 acres of beautiful parkland and gardens.

DINING OPTIONS

Starbucks, Waitrose, Eat in Restaurant, Burger King and KFC are all on-site at the hotel in Michaelwood, and many popular restaurants are just minutes away.

New Website

Be sure to check out the new website for all the latest information on Meandering Walking Series. This covers new paperback books, downloads, blogs and release dates for books later in 2015 or 2016.

http://johncoombes.wix.com/meandering-walks-2

Printed in Great Britain
by Amazon